THE SMART FAMILY'S GUIDE TO

Protecting An Aging Parent

from a Long Term Care Financial Crisis In California

BRENDA L. GEIGER, J.D.

BRADLEY ERDOSI, J.D.

GEIGER LAW OFFICE, P.C.
Geiger Law Office, P.C.
1917 Palomar Oaks Way, Suite 160
(760) 448-2220
www.geigerlawoffice.net
info@geigerlawoffice.net

LAW OFFICES OF BRADLEY S. ERDOSI
23101 Lake Center Drive, Suite 325
Lake Forest, CA 92630
(949) 261-5777
www.willsandtrustslaw.com

Published 2016.

Printed in the United States of America.

ISBN: 978-1-63385-114-6 [HARDBACK]
ISBN: 978-1-63385-120-7 [SOFTBACK]

Designed and published by

Word Association Publishers
205 Fifth Avenue
Tarentum, Pennsylvania 15084

www.wordassociation.com
1.800.827.7903

DISCLAIMER

This book is intended for educational purposes only and is not legal advice. For advice about your specific situation, please consult an experienced Elder Law Attorney.

CONTENTS

CHAPTER ONE

What is Elder Law for Long Term Care Planning?

Elder Law is an area of legal planning provided by specially trained attorneys who help aging clients and their families plan for the possibility of the need for long term care assistance, while also assisting in the preservation and protection of assets from the devastating cost of that care. This type of planning also seeks to avoid court involvement in the event of incapacity or death, by taking a proactive approach to estate planning, rather than reacting to a crisis event. Elder Law attorneys help aging adults plan to ensure access to future medical care, while ensuring the orderly passing of assets in an easy and efficient manner to children or other beneficiaries. Elder Law attorneys also help seniors ensure they have the proper documents in place to avoid possible future court involvement (through a Conservatorship or Probate), while ensuring that they continue to have a high quality of life until the end of their life.

Elder Law attorneys also help clients stay informed of law changes that may affect their plan and give advice regarding how to obtain public benefits, including Medi-Cal and VA benefits. A personalized plan addressing how to best use and manage the personal and financial resources available is key to proper long term care planning.

We have written this book to provide you with valuable information regarding the types of problems we help our clients solve. You may not have ever thought about or even thought to ask some of the questions answered in this book. Our purpose is to act as your guide to help you plan to protect yourself or a loved one so that you are not forced into the court process down the road or left wondering "how are we going to afford to pay for long term care?" This book is about ensuring your family's piece of mind.

Long-term care planning is the process of looking forward and deciding in advance how you or a loved one wants to be cared for and how that care will be paid for in the event of difficulty with living independently. As we all age, the risk of needing long-term care grows. Afflictions such as Alzheimer's Disease, dementia, stroke, heart attack, and broken hips from falls are just some of the most common reasons necessitating outside professional help or a nursing home stay.

Long-term care costs are rising at an alarming rate in California. It has become a major problem for many seniors. Some end up losing their life's savings, their homes, or both, paying for long term care left only to spend nearly every dime they have before government benefits are available. Statistics show that 60-70% of adults over 70 will need long term care at some point during their life. Studies show that the increased need for long term care is due to the fact that the average life expectancy has risen so dramatically in recent years.

The average cost per month for nursing home care statewide in California in 2015 is presently $7,628 (a number set annually by the State Medicaid Agency). However, the cost of long term care is often much greater in larger counties such as Los Angeles, San Francisco, Orange and San Diego Counties, where the monthly cost of nursing home care can be $10,000 or higher. According to the United States Administration on Aging, it is estimated that by 2037, the cost of a semi-private room in a skilled nursing facility will be over $31,000 per month.

In some cases, seniors are unable to get some or all of their medical needs met through traditional insurance.

Thus, Medi-Cal, V.A. Aid and Attendance Pension, or money from savings, children or other family members are the only options for ensuring full coverage for a long-term care stay in a nursing facility or to remain at home with assistance.

CHAPTER TWO

Proactive Planning for Long Term Care vs. Crisis Planning

In the big picture of planning for the real possibility of a long term care triggering event, there are two types of planning. There is the proactive approach where we plan ahead so that if and when a triggering event occurs, we have a lot more options to cover the expense of care and have the right people in place to help in the process of caring for an aging parent.

The next type of long term care planning is crisis planning. It's pretty much just like it sounds. We wait until a catastrophic event occurs (the stroke, heart attack, dementia, broken hip, etc.), and then we make a mad scramble to gain access to good health care, figure out how to pay for it and if still possible, put the right people in charge of the management of the finances and health care of an aging parent (sometimes required through court action).

Outside of the obvious difference between proactive and crisis planning of having either more or less options when the triggering event occurs, another big difference is the cost of the planning. Crisis planning costs significantly more from a legal planning fee perspective as well as the true cost for assisted living and medical care to the aging parent and/or his or her family.

Crisis planning costs significantly more from a legal planning fee perspective

Example of Proactive Planning:

To provide an example, imagine Aunt Betty who is 78. Aunt Betty often has lapses in her memory but all in all she is still in good health and able to take care of herself in her home. Aunt Betty has two adult children and several grandchildren but both of her children live out of state. Aunt Betty has a home in Southern California that is now worth close to $900,000 (she and her late husband purchased the home 40 years ago for $100,000). Betty also has a car, but it's not in very good condition. She also receives social security income of $1,000/month and a small pension of $1800/month from her late husband's company. Finally, she has a $100,000 CD at a local bank. Looking forward, there is a possibility that Betty may need in-home care or nursing care at a facility as a result of a dementia or Alzheimer's disease diagnosis. Betty's mother developed Alzheimer's in her early 80's and lived with the disease for 10 years.

Can Betty be helped? There are strategies and techniques that can be used to plan in advance how Betty would like to be cared for and how the cost of care will be covered. By pre-planning now, Aunt Betty may be able to preserve assets so that she does not end up in a crisis situation, requiring her to quickly spend down her assets in order to quality for government benefits. Aunt Betty also needs to make sure that she has an Advance Health Care Directive, HIPAA Authorization, "Expanded" Durable Power of Attorney for Finances, as well as one or more trusts to transfer assets to her children.

It is probably also a good idea for Aunt Betty to consider developing a good relationship with a geriatric care manager and Elder Law attorney to help her because her children live far away. Incapacity is not typically something that happens over night, but rather is a gradual process. Thus, in all circumstances, it is best to have someone there for an aging parent to rely on for support and advice, should more assistance down the road be required.

In Aunt Betty's case, her home is her largest asset. She really wants the home to be transferred to her children who grew up in the home. There are some important planning steps that should be undertaken to protect the family home from a later Medi-Cal recovery action. This can be accomplished through a special type of Irrevocable Trust (See Chapter 8 for more details). Other assets may be transferred to this special type of irrevocable trust as well. The interesting part of the trust is that we can have a trusted person in charge of that trust and that person can have the ability to make lifetime distributions from the trust to the beneficiaries of the trust (usually the trustmaker's children).

The sooner we do this however, the better. California has adopted the DRA (Deficit Reduction Act of 2005), but has not yet implemented it. New promulgated regulations have been introduced for public comment as of the publication date of this book. We are now awaiting approval and adoption of the new rules, thereby changing California Medicaid (Medi-Cal) law. One of the major effects of DRA implementation will be an expanded penalty period, including when a penalty period will begin as a result of gifts being made. Currently, if any penalty period is triggered, the penalty runs from the date the gift was made, not when an application for benefits under Medi-Cal is filed. That is expected to change when the DRA is implemented in California. The penalty period will begin on the date of application for Medi-Cal provided that such individual is otherwise eligible for Long Term Care Medi-Cal. This is a huge change from the current law and will severely restrict and affect new Medi-Cal applicants. This will impact many unknowing seniors who make gifts to family members and who will need nursing home care in the future. For example, if Aunt Betty made a gift to an irrevocable trust for her children that triggered a 10 month penalty period right now, (current law in California), the penalty period would run from the date she made the gift and it would expire in 10 months. Under the new proposed rules, if Betty applied for benefits even 59 months from now, the 10 month penalty period would begin at that point in time, making her ineligible for Medi-Cal for 10 months from the date she applied. Therefore, doing the planning now has a huge advantage under the current set of rules.

There are many other strategies and techniques to help aid a family in planning for long-term care. Veterans benefits may also may be a part of the planning process for long term care. But, careful planning is required when looking at the big picture. The rules for Medi-Cal and for VA benefits are very different. One could obtain VA benefits and inadvertently make him/her ineligible for Medi-Cal which could end up providing an aging adult with better overall coverage. It is best to speak with an accredited VA attorney versed in Medi-Cal and Veterans Benefits before doing anything that would jeopardize future benefits. For more on planning for Veteran's benefits, see Chapters 7 to 9 of this book.

Example of Crisis Planning:

Imagine John. John worked for a phone company for 45 years. John has been retired for about 15 years and will soon be 80 years old. John's wife Emma died 10 years ago from a long battle with breast cancer. Unfortunately, her medical bills fighting the cancer chewed up much of John and Emma's savings. John has two children. His daughter Sara lives about 40 miles from John and his son Tom lives out of state with his family.

John has slowed down a lot in the last year or two and his balance isn't what it used to be. John has high blood pressure and has had two stents put in over the last year. His daughter Sara is very concerned about what will happen if John has a stroke or falls.

John still lives at home alone, the home he's owned for 40 years in San Diego. John and Emma paid $30,000 for their home in 1975 and have put about $20,000 into the home since then. Now, the house is worth about $850,000.

John has about $160,000 in his savings account and has a monthly income of about $3500 from his pension and Social Security together. John does not have any long-term care insurance, but he does have a basic estate plan in place. The estate plan however was drafted over 20 years ago and John and Emma never updated their plan. There have been many changes in the law and in John and Emma's financial situation since the trust was drafted 20 years ago.

John's daughter is married with two children and is a nurse at a local hospital. She checks in on John as often as she can with her busy work schedule and family life, but it's a challenge. She's recently become quite worried about John's health because he's had a couple of falls and he had two stents put in last year. He's also become more forgetful in the last six months.

Then, Sara got a call from John's doctor that he had a major fall and is in the hospital. John broke his hip in the fall. John needs surgery to repair his broken hip but there is a possibility of further memory loss if he's put under anesthesia to repair his broken hip and it could render him legally incapacitated and unable to sign documents.

Because Sara is a nurse in the emergency room, she has been exposed to some training on qualifying for government benefits for long term care stays. Though she's not an expert, she knows enough to contact a local elder law attorney that she has referred past patients of the hospital to.

Do to the emergency nature of the situation, Sara was able to get an appointment with the attorney the next day. The attorney suggested that John execute a special type of immediate Power of Attorney, a new Advance Health Care Directive and a HIPAA Authorization to Release Medical Information. She also recommended that John set up an irrevocable trust and transfer his home to it, all before he goes in for surgery in two days.

The need to do this prior to the surgery is critical because John may come out of the surgery lacking the requisite capacity to do any legal planning and Sara and her brother could wind up having to spend nearly all of John's savings before he could qualify for any government benefits if needed. They could also wind up needing to get him under a conservatorship because his existing documents are so old. The attorney was able to visit with John in the hospital right away to make sure that his wishes were met. But this ended up costing John and his children significantly more than if they had planned ahead.

Fortunately, the attorney was able to turn around drafting of the documents by moving clients around to accommodate the emergency situation and set up the irrevocable trust plan before John's surgery. The attorney also set up a strategic gifting plan through Sara as John's Power of Attorney agent to move some of John's assets into the irrevocable trust so that the family could preserve some of John's assets in a protected way in case he became incapacitated or had a lengthy stay in the skilled nursing facility. The home is now safe from a future Medi-Cal recovery action.

If John and Sara had planned ahead in advance of this crisis, they could have protected all of his assets and spent a lot less to get that done.

CHAPTER THREE

What Documents Should be Part of the Estate Plan

if an Aging Parent Becomes Unable to Make Financial or Medical Decisions?

Planning for the possibility of incapacity is critical for anyone but especially for an aging parent. Without proper planning in advance, many adult children are forced to file a court action to obtain conservatorship over their parent when incapacity strikes.

You can avoid this expensive and burdensome process by having certain documents as part of your parent's estate plan. The key documents are a Trust, Statutory Power of Attorney, Expanded Durable Power of Attorney, Advance Healthcare Directive, and a HIPAA Authorization for Release of Medical Information.

First, having a Trust is key to the future management of assets in the event of incapacity (whether it be a temporary or a permanent incapacity). Revocable Trusts are

Trusts which are amendable by the person creating the Trust. The assets inside the Revocable Trust are generally part of the estate at death when calculating whether there is an estate tax. There are many benefits to the use of revocable Trusts. The most commonly known is the ability to avoid a probate court action. Revocable Trusts are also great tools to manage property in the event of incapacity. However, assets placed into a Revocable Trust will not be protected in the event it becomes necessary to qualify a parent for Medicaid (Medi-Cal in California) or prevent an Estate Recovery action by the state if benefits are obtained.

Irrevocable Trusts on the other hand are not amendable, with a few minor exceptions. In the context of planning for long term care, these types of Trusts can be powerful asset preservation vehicles so long as there are trusted children or other family members or friends that are willing to be a part of the plan and the trust is properly drafted. Irrevocable Trusts are commonly utilized in high net-worth estates to reduce or eliminate estate tax exposure. Today however, we have borrowed many of the strategies from high net-worth estate planning to achieve asset preservation for more modest estates to pre-plan for the possibility of a future long term care need and more options in accessing skilled nursing benefits.

To bring this concept to life, imagine the case of Uncle Bob. Uncle Bob has been a widow for five years. He is now 79 years old and he has 2 adult children. Bob's mother passed away at the age of 89 from Alzheimer's disease. Now, Bob is starting to exhibit early warning signs of the disease. Bob's daughter, Linda, is very concerned about her father and wants to make sure he is happy, healthy and secure. Bob is recognizing his own deficits and is worried about the future and how he is going to pay for his long term care. Both of his children work full time and have children of their own. Bob owns a home in Newport Beach near the coast that he has lived in for 35 years. His home is now worth $800,000 and Bob has about $200,000 in liquid assets. Bob does not want to have to sell his home immediately in the event he needs funds to pay for his care (including skilled nursing care). In this case, an irrevocable trust (also sometimes referred to as Medicaid Trust) can provide an efficient solution and prevent a future Medi-Cal estate recovery action, while maintaining many of the tax benefits as though Bob owned the home in his own name (see Chapter 8 for more details on this special type of irrevocable trust).

After consulting with his attorney, Bob and his daughter Linda, have decided that an irrevocable trust is an ideal solution for him. He decides to transfer his home by gift to the trust. Because of the way the trust is drafted, Bob can maintain his Proposition 13 property tax basis he has in his home and is still able to apply his Internal Revenue Code Section 121 federal capital gains exemption should his home be sold inside the trust while he's still alive. The IRC Section 121 Exemption, as it is commonly called, allows a single person to exclude up to $250,000 of capital gains ($500,000 for married couples) on the sale of a primary residence resided in for 2 of the last 5 years prior to the sale as a primary residence. Bob also decides that he'd like to move $100,000 of his liquid assets to the trust in order to reduce the Medi-Cal ineligibility penalty period should he need to immediately apply for benefits. For Medi-Cal eligibility, we devised a gifting strategy to the trust that actually triggered no ineligibility period. Bob wants to keep the other $100,000 in his Revocable Trust that he can use for his lifestyle and as a rainy day emergency fund. He has approximately $3,000 a month in income from Social Security and his $1000 a month pension, which is all he needs for his lifestyle at this point in time.

Bob is very close to both of his children, but Linda has been the one who is most involved with Bob's health-care and well-being. Bob has decided that he would like Linda to serve as Trustee of the new Irrevocable Trust and as co-trustee with him on his Revocable Trust. Bob's son John is the successor Trustee after Linda on his Revocable Trust and will serve as a successor Trustee after Linda on Bob's Irrevocable Trust.

After Bob's home and the $100,000 are transferred to Bob's Irrevocable Trust, Linda will then manage the property inside the Trust. Bob decided to list both Linda and John as lifetime beneficiaries and death time beneficiaries. What this means is that during Bob's lifetime, Linda, as Trustee, has the authority to make distributions of trust principal and income to both John and herself. Bob is <u>not</u> a beneficiary of his Irrevocable Trust. Remember, by transferring the home and the $100,000 to the Irrevocable Trust, a gift was made to his children through the Irrevocable Trust and he no longer owns that property. The children are free to do what they wish with the trust assets and in a good family such as Bob's, one might expect that Linda and John will look out for Bob's best interest down the road should he ever need them to.

Although we have tried to make this look like a simple transaction, there are many details and considerations that go into the design of this type of trust, as well as the gifting strategy to this trust. It is very important that you seek appropriate legal counsel to accomplish this transaction.

The next document Bob needs to make sure is part of his plan is a Durable Power of Attorney. For our clients, we prepare two financial Power of Attorney documents. The first one is a Statutory Durable Power of Attorney and the other is an Expanded Durable Power of Attorney. We like to have both working together because each has a tactical advantage. The Statutory Power of Attorney is helpful because if a bank or financial institution refuses to accept it, they could be liable for attorney's fees and damages if they fail to accept California's statutory document.

The Expanded Durable Power of Attorney on the other hand helps us to plan for Medi-Cal planning and qualification, disclaimer planning, and advanced estate planning just to name a few (should the need arise in the future and Bob does not have legal capacity to sign documents or move his assets into an irrevocable trust). It is more expanded in terms of what it can do than the Statutory Form Power of Attorney, so we like to have both in place in all estate plans. It may also be advisable to make both of these Power of Attorney documents active immediately instead of springing into activity at incapacity when we have an elder parent we are trying to protect. If a springing Power of Attorney is opted for, an Incapacity Declaration by one or more doctors will likely be required depending upon how the document is drafted.

The last two documents that are critical to have in the estate plan are the Advance Health Care Directive and the HIPAA Authorization. The Advance Health Care Directive is California's statutory form for nominating an agent to make medical decisions for you if you cannot, the election for end of life decisions and election for being an organ donor. It is important to list two or three agents in the order in which you would like them to serve just in case your first choice is unable or unwilling to act. The HIPAA Authorization allows you to give certain people access to your medical status or documents, as well as to talk with your doctor about your health care options or capacity. It can help a family member discover if and where you have been admitted to a hospital and allow your attorney to talk with your doctor about your capacity to sign documents. The Advance Health Care Directive is governed by state law and involves who can make medical decisions for you. The HIPAA Authorization is federal law and governs the release of medical information to authorized parties.

Taking all of these documents listed above together, if the documents are well crafted, they make for a solid estate plan to ensure a family does not need to procure court involvement to help an aging parent down the road.

All of these documents together, make for a solid estate plan to ensure a family does not need to procure court involvement

CHAPTER FOUR

What is the Difference Between MediCare and Medi-Cal?

Medi-Cal is California's implementation of the Federal Medicaid health care program. It is different from Medicare because Medicare is an entitlement program for those that have paid into the system by working in the United States. Medi-Cal by contrast is California's implementation of the Federal Medicaid laws and is based on financial need. One must qualify for Medi-Cal based on his or her specific financial situation in order to be covered for benefits.

Medi-Cal pays for a variety of medical services for children and adults with limited income and resources. The Medi-Cal system is paid for by federal and state taxes. If you are determined to be eligible, you can get Medi-Cal as long as you continue to meet the eligibility requirements. This is why potential inheritances, gifts to the person on Medi-Cal or extra income from work can be problematic for someone on Medi-Cal.

Medicare is an entitlement program that pays for many medical expenses for those 65 or older or with certain disabilities. Medicare can cover up to 100 days of skilled nursing care, but rarely does. Medicare Part A covers hospitalization, home health care and limited nursing home care. Part A also covers hospice care for terminal illness. Medicare beneficiaries also pay a deductible for hospital care. Additionally, there may be a required payment for some share of cost after the 20th day in a nursing home. However, there are no deductibles or other share of cost payments due for home health and hospice care. It is important to note that Medicare skilled nursing home care coverage is limited to 100 days (with some of that time requiring a co-pay). Accordingly, those utilizing this benefit often need to turn to other sources for payment for the co-pay or a stay over 100 days, which could include Medi-Cal, long term care insurance or self-paying from personal funds.

Medicare Part B covers your doctor's visits, some medical equipment, home health care, lab tests, and some preventative services. Part B generally pays up to 80% of approved expenses. You are responsible for the other 20% along with any uncovered expenses and an annual deductible. There is no cost sharing for some preventative services and home health care. Part B is optional. You will need to pay a monthly premium for the coverage and Part B can be withheld from your Social Security check.

Many Medicare recipients purchase separate insurance to cover themselves for the deductibles on Part A and Part B. These policies are typically called "Medigap" or "Medicare supplemental policies."

One must qualify for Medi-Cal based on his or her specific financial situation in order to be covered for benefits.

CHAPTER FIVE

What Are the Qualification Requirements for Long Term Care Medi-Cal Benefits?

Medi-Cal is California's version of the Federal Medicaid program. The Medi-Cal program is administered by the California Department of Health Care Services. For adults over 65 who qualify, Medi-Cal will pay for the costs of a skilled nursing home care stay, which in California can average between $7,000 to $12,000 (or more for extreme care needs), for those paying with private funds.

The options for paying for the cost of nursing home care are:

1. Medicare – However, Medicare will only cover skilled nursing home care for a very limited amount of time and with a co-pay after day 20.

2. Long Term Care Insurance – For those who have purchased long term care insurance, the amount covered will be determined by the specific terms of the policy (and may not cover it all).

3. Private Pay – A person in a skilled nursing home will use savings to pay the monthly costs of care.

4. Medi-Cal – California's Medi-Cal program will pay for the nursing home care shortfall between the income of the recipient and the cost of care of the facility.

The Medi-Cal program will pay for the cost of nursing home care for those 65 and over who meet the financial and medical necessity qualifications of the program. Since Medi-Cal is a needs-based program, the amount of the assets that a person can have to qualify for benefits is limited. The financial requirements differ for a single person and a married couple. Generally, the financial requirements are as follows:

1. The applicant (if single) cannot own more than $2,000 in total assets. (See exempt and non-countable assets below).
2. Monthly income less than the cost of the skilled nursing facility care.

In determining financial eligibility, California applies an assets cap test. Certain assets are exempt or are non-countable for the assets calculation (at present). Those assets include:

- the personal residence (unlimited value under current law); this will be changed once the DRA proposed regulations go into effect; under the new rules, the estimated equity limit will be somewhere between $750,000 to $828,000, indexed annually for inflation
- one automobile
- retirement plans in active pay out status
- certain Medi-Cal approved annuities
- personal property
- pre-paid burial contracts

Any other assets owned by the applicant must not exceed $2,000 in order to qualify for nursing home Medi-Cal. What this means is that the applicant must not own more than $2,000 at the time of application in order to qualify. Annual recertification is required and the same rules apply.

In California, in order to be eligible for Medi-Cal, an individual must also be determined to be "medically needy" by the Medicaid Office and either 65 or over or determined eligible through disability. Medically needy involves impairment of some or all of the acts of daily living (ADLs). The acts of daily living are eating, bathing, toileting, dressing, and transferring. Typically, we need to see a majority of these ADLs medically impaired for approval of the Medi-Cal application.

The rules for qualification when the applicant for Medi-Cal is married are slightly different. Medi-Cal will require disclosure of both spouses' income and assets at the time of application for just one spouse to receive benefits.

In the planning for qualification of an ill spouse, there is a "Community Spouse Resource Allowance" (CSRA). In California, the community spouse may keep up to a maximum of $119,220 (in 2015) in his or her own name and still get their ill spouse qualified for Medi-Cal.

- The income of the community spouse is not counted in determining the Medi-Cal applicant's eligibility but the ill spouse's income (or a portion of it) will need to be given to the selected Skilled Nursing Facility (SNF) and the facility back bills Medi-Cal for the balance.
- What if most of the couple's income is in the name of the ill spouse and the community spouse's income is not enough to live on?
  - The community spouse could be entitled to some or all of the monthly income of the ill spouse.
  - The Minimum Monthly Maintenance Needs Allowance (MMMNA) is calculated for each community "well" spouse according to a formula based on housing costs.
  - The MMMNA may range from a low of $1,966.25 to a high of $2,980.50 a month in California (in 2015).

- California's Medi-Cal Estate Recovery Program
  - There is no limit to the amount that can be billed against the Medi-Cal recipient's assets by the state.
  - Estate Recovery seeks a **100% payback** of whatever each state determines are expenses they want to recover for. Medi-Cal is not so much an insurance program but rather it is a loan against the estate.
- With careful planning, preservation of some or all of an aging parent's assets is possible while meeting the Medi-Cal asset limit.
- One of the ways we can protect an aging parent's assets from a Medi-Cal recovery action is through an Irrevocable Trust or also commonly called a Medicaid Trust (*see* Chapter 8).
  - A family can avoid the need to spend down all of the assets of an aging parent in order to qualify for Medi-Cal if it ever becomes necessary by planning ahead.

Loved ones can be lifetime beneficiaries of the irrevocable trust and do what they wish with the assets of this special trust.

How the Trust Works:

1. Assets are transferred to the irrevocable trust with a family member or other trusted person acting as Trustee (this cannot be the aging parent acting as the Trustee).
2. The Trustee is in charge of managing and guarding the assets in the irrevocable trust.
3. After assets are transferred into the Irrevocable Trust, they can only later be distributed to the named lifetime beneficiaries of the trust by the Trustee.
4. The property now belongs to the trust and is no longer considered part of the aging parent's assets for Medi-Cal asset calculations (with adherence to some specific rules).
5. The benefits of the irrevocable trust are to allow families or individuals to:
   - ✓ Protect their assets from the cost of long-term care

- ✓ Leave money now and at death to children or charities
- ✓ Provide creditor protection for beneficiaries after the death of an aging parent
- ✓ Provide more flexibility and options if and when a long term crisis arises
- ✓ Protect the assets now from the creditors of the beneficiaries
- ✓ Maintain Section 121 Exclusion from capital gains on a primary residence
- ✓ Maintain step-up in basis on assets on the death of the aging parent

6. The lifetime beneficiaries may do what they wish with the distributions from the trust which are tax free including indirectly augmenting the medical care and treatment of an aging parent. The trust is also what we call a "Grantor" trust, which means that the income taxes are attributable to the person who created the trust (the aging parent).

7. We are typically not concerned about estate tax issues in these types of planning situations because we are not dealing with assets over the federal estate tax exemption limit of $5,430,000 (2015). If the aging parent has more than $5,000,000, they are more than likely going to be able to pay for future long term care.

Issues Solved by the Use of an Irrevocable Trust

1. Creditor Protection: The person who receives the assets could die, become estranged, get divorced, invest badly, spend the money, or even lose the money to "their" creditors. Thus, by transferring the assets into this special type of irrevocable trust, these issues are avoided.

2. Continued control by a trusted family member: The individual who creates and funds an irrevocable trust can establish the rules of the trust and who the Trustees will be and who the lifetime and death-time beneficiaries will be. The aging parent creating this trust can also retain the right to reside in

their primary residence that is transferred to the trust rent free.

3. Prevention of an Estate Recovery Action by the state of California: If the exempt family home is transferred to the Irrevocable Trust and the aging parent later goes on Medi-Cal benefits, because the home is not in his or her name, the State will not be able to recover against the home for a payback. This only includes a primary residence that we reserve the right to live in or have an “intention” to return to which can be done in the irrevocable trust (currently there is no equity limit in California, but upon implementation of the new proposed regulations, it will be restricted most likely to $828,000 for a single person but could be as low at $750,000).

4. Preservation of the step-up in basis of the home at the death of the Grantor: If an asset is subject to gain upon sale (i.e. the Grantor’s primary residence) is retained in the trust until the death of the Grantor, the asset can still receive a step-up in basis (this could be a huge capital gains tax savings on a family

home where the Grantor has a very low basis in the home relative to its fair market value upon sale). The trust can be drafted with special language making it a "Grantor" trust to allow for the step-up in tax basis. The Tax ID of the trust is the Grantor's social security number. If the aging parent were to directly "gift" their home to a child, the original basis would travel with the home and the child may experience a large capital gains tax upon sale.

5. Retention of the Section 121 exclusion from gain: If the family home is sold within the Trust by the Trustee, special language can be added to the trust allowing for the exclusion from gain of $250,000 for an individual or $500,000 for a married couple, provided the Grantor lived in the home 2 of the last 5 years.

6. Protection from a beneficiary's creditors: Using an irrevocable trust also avoids the risk that a beneficiary could die and that the funds are inherited by the beneficiary's heirs or his or her estate creditors. Additionally, this protects the assets from a beneficiary's divorce, lawsuit, bankruptcy, or to another creditor.

7. An irrevocable trust provides more options for planning should a later crisis occur: If a crisis strikes, having all or a portion of the Grantor's assets in an irrevocable trust allows for faster access to needed Medi-Cal services.

    - The family, typically the children, may withdraw funds from the trust for HEMS purposes (the beneficiary's Health, Education, Maintenance and Support).

    - If the beneficiary wishes to use his or her own funds from their own bank account to supplement the care and treatment of an ill parent, that is in their discretion.

    - The irrevocable trust strategy should be reserved only for parent/child or other family relationships that are good ones and have caring children. Our primary concern here is the comfort and medical care of the aging parent.

8. It's currently easier to do planning in California (which will become much more difficult when the DRA proposed regulations become law). California is currently

one of the easiest states to do Medicaid pre-planning in due to the lack of implementation of the DRA (Deficit Reduction Act) regulations which equates to earlier access to needed medical services.

- Currently, stacked gifts to an irrevocable trust is possible with little or no penalty and the family home is currently an exempt transfer (no look back period on the home if transferred to a properly drafted irrevocable trust).
- The State of California proposed DRA regulations over 2 years ago. We thought these would be implemented already. It's likely to happen anytime now.
- The new major changes: (1) the penalty period for gifts will run from date of application (if a gift is made within 5 years of application, it needs to be disclosed on the Medi-Cal application. Currently, a triggered penalty runs from the date the gift is made). (2) The equity cap on the family home. It will likely be between $750,000 to $828,000 - it's not clear yet.

Currently, the home exemption is unlimited. Therefore, creation of an irrevocable trust and transferring the family home to an irrevocable trust are strongly advised for families wanting to protect that asset.

CHAPTER SIX

One Spouse is Already in a Nursing Home, is it Too Late to Plan for Long Term Care?

Often times, it is necessary for a spouse to go into a nursing home, and the at-home well spouse believes that there is nothing he or she can do in order to protect and preserve their assets. In this situation, although dire, there are still planning opportunities.

This type of planning is considered "crisis planning." Crisis planning is much different than pre-planning, which is planning for long-term care before a loved one enters a nursing home or has a debilitating event which prevents him or her from doing any planning (such as a stroke or dementia that causes incapacity).

When engaging in pre-planning for long-term care asset preservation, a single individual or married couple can protect and preserve nearly all of their assets. Conversely, when a single individual or one spouse is already in a nursing home, it is nearly impossible to save all of their assets. However, regardless of how far along in the "crisis," it is still possible to protect and preserve some assets. Thus, regardless of the situation, it is never too late to plan.

One of the biggest mistakes in planning for long-term care is the erroneous belief that it is too late to plan.

The strategies available in crisis planning are far more limited than when doing pre-planning for long-term care. An additional issue that arises in crisis planning is the increased likelihood that the spouse who has been admitted to the nursing home lacks the legal mental capacity to engage in any sort of planning. In this situation, often times the only available solution for the well spouse (also called an "at-home or community spouse") to plan for all of the assets is to go to court through a procedure commonly referred to as a California Probate Code Section 3100 Petition. However, with a special type of comprehensive durable power of attorney, enabling the at-home spouse to engage in financial long term care planning, this court procedure may be averted and a lot of time and money can be saved.

California Probate Code Section 3100 Petition

A petition under California Probate Code Section 3100 is a proceeding wherein one spouse lacks the legal capacity to engage in any sort of legal transaction. In this situation, California Probate Code Section 3100 allows the spouse with capacity to petition the court to approve a particular and proposed transaction on behalf of the spouse lacking capacity. A 3100 petition is often times a very effective tool for having assets which are titled in both spouses' names to be transferred to the spouse who has capacity. Upon a successful 3100 petition and appropriate court order, the spouse with capacity may then engage in long-term care planning.

Additionally, California Probate Code Section 3100 and related sections, may allow for the well spouse to petition the court to increase the Community Spouse Resource Allowance and/or direct that some of the income of the spouse in the nursing home be directed to the community spouse. However, there are several counties in California which will not authorize such a transaction (*i.e.*, at the time of this publication, Orange County courts do not authorize an increase in the Community Spouse Resource Allowance).

Transfers Between Spouses

Currently, there is no penalty for transfers of assets between spouses, even if one spouse is in a nursing home. Thus, if a spouse has capacity or there is a valid POA allowing it, a spouse in a nursing home may transfer all of his or her assets to the at-home spouse without any penalty. Once this is accomplished, the at-home spouse may engage in certain strategies in order to plan to protect assets from the devastating costs of long-term care.

The above discussion is based on the current state of the law in California. Of course, when the Deficit Reduction Act of 2005 becomes effective in California, a new analysis must be done based upon the law as it is enacted and the regulations which interpret it. Planning now is strongly advised.

CHAPTER SEVEN

Qualifying for VA Benefits: Is This Difficult to Do?

This chapter will focus on differentiating the most common types of monetary veteran's benefits and outlining what is involved in applying for those benefits.

The first type of benefit is disability compensation. Disability compensation is paid to a veteran as a result of injuries or diseases that were caused by or made worse by active military service. The veteran's injury is rated as a percentage of loss (i.e.10%, 20%, 100% disabled).

The second most common type of veteran's benefit is the non-service connected pension. The pension is paid to wartime veterans or surviving spouses of wartime veterans who qualify. Qualification for a non-service connected pension is a means based program qualification based on "financial" need. This benefit is paid to wartime veterans (or spouses of veterans) with limited or no income that are age 65 or older, (or, if under 65 permanently and totally disabled). Certain veterans may be entitled to Aid and Attendance or housebound benefits. The Aid and Attendance benefits are paid in addition to the basic pension rate.

The eligibility requirements for the Basic Pension are that (1) the veteran is age 65 or older (or is permanently and totally disabled, not due to the veteran's own willful misconduct); (2) discharged from service under conditions other than dishonorable; (3) served at least 90 days of active military service and 1 day of which was during a war time period (if the veteran entered active duty after September 7, 1980, generally you must have served at least 24 months or the full period for which called or ordered to active duty-there are some exceptions to this rule); (4) net worth is not excessive (note: there is no set limit but we have seen people with as little as $30,000 be denied and people with as much of $120,000 in assets be approved); and (5) the countable family income is below a yearly limit set by law.

Eligibility Requirement No. 1:

The veteran must be 65 or older, or "permanently and totally disabled" (38 CFR §3.3 (a)(3)(vi)). Generally, the veteran is considered permanently and totally disabled if the veteran is a patient in a nursing home for long-term care because of disability or disabled as determined by the Commissioner of Social Security for purposes of any benefits administered by the Commissioner. Being unemployable as a result of disability reasonably certain to continue throughout the life of the person may also meet this requirement.

Eligibility Requirement No. 2:

The second eligibility requirement is the discharge requirement. The veteran must have been discharged from service under conditions other than a dishonorable discharge. Under 38 CFR 3.1(d), "*Veteran* means a person who served in active military, naval, or air service and who was discharged or released under conditions other than dishonorable."

Eligibility Requirement No. 3:

The third eligibility requirement is the service requirement. If the veteran entered service prior to September 7, 1980, the veteran must have served at least 90 days of consecutive active military service 1 day of which was during a war time period. For exceptions to 90 days of consecutive active duty service, see 38CFR §3.3. If the veteran entered service after September 7, 1980, the veteran must have served a minimum of 24 months of continuous active duty or the full period for which a person was called or ordered to active duty. The veteran is excepted from the 24 month requirement if he or she served at least one day of wartime service and was discharged for a service connected disability (38 CFR §3.3(a)(3)).

Eligibility Requirement No. 4:

The fourth requirement is a limited net worth. The veteran or spouse must have a limited net worth, which is set forth in 38 CFR 3.274 as follows:"*Pension shall be denied or discontinued when the corpus of the estate of the veteran, and of the veteran's spouse, are such that under all the circumstances, including consideration of the annual income of the veteran, the veteran's spouse, and the veteran's children, it is reasonable that some part of the corpus of such estates be consumed for the veteran's maintenance."*

So, what is the criteria for determining net worth under 38 CFR §3.275? The VA says that there is no set limit on how much net worth a veteran and his or her dependents can have, but net worth cannot be excessive. The decision as to whether a claimant's net worth is excessive depends on the facts of each individual case. The VA will determine if a claimant's assets are sufficiently large enough that the claimant could live off these assets for a reasonable period of time. The VA's needs-based programs are not intended to protect substantial assets or build up an estate for the benefit of heirs.

The terms corpus of estate and net worth mean the market value, less mortgages or other encumbrances, of all real and personal property owned by the claimant, except the claimant's dwelling (single family unit), including a reasonable lot area, and personal effects suitable to and consistent with the claimant's reasonable mode of life. Net worth does not include normal household objects and possessions, or a motor vehicle used for family transportation.

There is a misconception out there that the "magic" qualification limit on assets is $80,000. This is a myth. Must a claimant have less than $80,000 to qualify? No! But net worth should be minimal. Where does the $80,000 limit come from? The VA's adjudication manual (M21-1MR, Part V, Subpart iii, Chapter 1, Section J 70) states that a formal administrative net worth decision is required if the beneficiary has a net worth of $80,000 or more, whether or not net worth bars entitlement or net worth (of any amount) bars entitlement.

So, just what is excessive net worth? There is no specific dollar amount that can be identified as excessive net worth. What constitutes excessive net worth is a question of fact or resolution after considering the facts and circumstances in each case. A number of variables must be taken into consideration when making a net worth determination. Some of the factors to consider include (1) income from other sources; (2) family expenses; (3) the claimant's life expectancy; and (4) how convertible the assets in the net worth are to being converted to cash.

In general, the older the claimant is, the less assets will be needed to meet his or her financial needs until his or her death. The VA pension program is not intended to protect substantial assets or build up a claimant's estate for the benefit of his or her heirs. So, what this means is that in general, the older you are, the less in general that the VA is going to let you have in your total net worth in order to qualify for Aid & Attendance benefits.

> The older the claimant is, the less assets will be needed to meet his or her financial needs until his or her death.

Eligibility Requirement No. 5:

The last eligibility requirement is the income requirement. The VA calculates income differently than the IRS and Medi-Cal. The VA calculates income by the claimant's gross monthly household income. There are things that get deducted from that number. Out-of-pocket unreimbursed medical expenses (UMEs) reduce the income almost dollar-for-dollar (there is a slight deductible). When the UMEs are subtracted from the income, you have IVAP, or Income for VA Purposes. What we are looking for to qualify is an IVAP of zero or close to it.

There are different types of income. There is one-time income or lump sum receipt of income (receipt of income may occur more than once each year, but each receipt is a separate event). An example is an inheritance. There is also recurring income that is received on regular basis and in regular amounts. An example of that would be a pension, IRA required minimum distribution or Social Security payments. There is also irregular income which is received several times a year, but at irregular times or in irregular amounts. An example of this might be interest income or occasional employment earnings.

As stated above, unreimbursed medical expenses (UMEs) reduce gross income. The veteran must have actually paid the expense. At the time of application, the veteran or spouse claimant must report UMEs which will be expected and recurring over the next 12 months. UMEs arc subject to a deductible equal to 5% of the base pension rate.

So, what are some common UMEs? Assisted living facility expenses are a common UME provided a doctor certifies that a "protective environment" is necessary. Some other common UMEs are Medicare premiums, caregiver expenses, long term care insurance premiums, health insurance premiums, and prescription drugs necessary for recurring conditions and expected to last for an indefinite period of time.

2015 Service Pension rates

(Including Aid and Attendance Benefit)

Category	Maximum Annual Pension Rate	Monthly MAPR
Service Pension	$12,867	$1,072
With one dependent	$16,851	$1,404
Housebound	$15,725	$1,310
With one dependent	$19,709	$1,642
Aid & Attendance	$21,466	$1,788
With one dependent	$25,447	$2120
For each additional dependent child	$2,198	$183

2015 Death Pension rates

(Including Aid and Attendance Benefit)

Category	Maximum Annual Pension Rate	Monthly MAPR
Service Pension	$8,629	$719
With one dependent	$11,296	$941
Housebound	$10,547	$864
With one dependent	$13,209	$1,101
Aid & Attendance	$13,794	$1,149
With one dependent	$16,455	$1,413
For each additional dependent child	$2,198	$183

There are currently no transfer penalties for VA benefits for transfers prior to application like there are for Medi-Cal benefits. However, transfers to a relative living in the residence will not reduce net worth. The applicant must relinquish all rights of ownership in the asset transferred. Life estates are ignored by the VA for net worth purposes. Note: There are new regulations that have been recently proposed, but yet to be enacted as of the date of this publication in 2015.

Possible Changes to VA Pension/Aid and Attendance Program?

Recently, the Department of Veteran's Affairs has issued proposed regulations, intending to change the Code of Federal Regulations and certain rules surrounding qualification for Veteran's Pension, Survivor's Pension, and Aid and Attendance Benefits. According to the VA, these proposed rules are aimed to "fill gaps" regarding perceived ambiguities in current law.

An additional purpose of these proposed rules, according to the VA, is to promote consistent decisions and uniformity, to reduce the opportunities for financial advisors to restructure assets to make a Veteran or spouse appear indigent, and make the rules consistent with penalties for other needs-based benefits. In summary, the proposed rules are intended to:

- Establish a clear net worth limit.
- Describe how the VA calculates assets.
- Establish a presumption, absent clear and convincing evidence, that asset transfers made 36 months prior to application, were made to establish pension entitlement.
- Creates a penalty period not to exceed 10 years.
- Defines certain authorized deductible medical expenses (UMEs).
- Centralizes all statutory exclusions from income and assets.
- Extends the reduction of pension to $90 for certain beneficiaries receiving Medicaid in a nursing home.

Proposed Rule 38 CFR 3.274 – Establishes a clear net worth limit.

Under the new proposed rules, the VA is intending to limit net worth to the maximum Community Spouse Resource Allowance (CSRA) established for Medicaid purposes. This amount in 2015 is currently $119,220, and will be indexed for inflation. In addition to the maximum CSRA, net worth will be increased by a claimant's annual income.

Proposed Rule 38 CFR 3.276, 3.275 – How the VA calculates assets.

Currently, the VA excludes from the calculation of net worth a claimant's residence and reasonable lot area. The new proposed regulations intend to limit this exclusion to a residence, plus a lot area not to exceed two acres. If the residence is sold, the sale of the residence may disqualify the Veteran unless the money is used to purchase another residence within the calendar year of sale. On a brighter note, the VA has proposed that a residence will continue to be excluded in the calculation of net worth, even if the claimant resides in a skilled nursing facility, residential care facility, assisted living facility, or relative's home.

Proposed Rule 38 CFR 3.276 –
How the VA penalizes asset transfers.

The VA is intending to establish a look-back period and penalize asset transfers prior to application. The new proposed rule establishes a presumption that transfers made within 36 months of application will cause disqualification. This presumption can only be overcome by clear and convincing evidence. There are no opportunities to claim hardship and the maximum penalty period is proposed to be 10 years.

The VA intends to calculate the penalty period as follows:

> Value of the covered asset transferred DIVIDED BY the Maximum Annual Pension Rate

Once this calculation is made, the VA will round down to the nearest whole number to determine the months of qualification.

This calculation creates differing penalty periods for a Veteran who is married than it would for a single Veteran and a surviving spouse. By way of example, assuming $50,000 in assets were transferred during the 36 month look-back period, the penalty period would be calculated as follows based on 2015 numbers:

> Married Veteran: $50,000 ÷ $2,120 = 23 months of penalty
>
> Single Veteran: $50,000 ÷ $1,788 = 27 months of penalty
>
> Surviving Spouse: $50,000 ÷ $1,149 = 43 months of penalty

As can be seen from the example above, a transfer of $50,000 by a surviving spouse of a veteran will cause a disqualification period nearly 20 months greater than the same gift by a veteran applying for pension. The proposed rules can be found at:

http://www.gpo.gov/fdsys/pkg/FR-2015-01-23/pdf/2015-00297.pdf

CHAPTER EIGHT

What is an Irrevocable Medicaid Protection Trust?

An Irrevocable Medicaid Protection Trust is a type of irrevocable trust used in planning ahead for possible long term care needs. Many of the characteristics of an intentionally defective trust (for tax purposes) that have been borrowed from trusts commonly used in high net worth planning to mitigate estate taxes have been utilized in this unique trust. The purpose of the trust is to protect assets from being counted for Medicaid benefits for long term care (should the need arise in the future) and to allow the lifetime beneficiaries of the trust to access trust funds as needed. Because the assets are held in trust by a Trustee, they can also be protected from the beneficiary's creditors, divorcing spouse, death, or bankruptcy.

In the trust, there should be no reservation of principal or income to go to the Grantor as a beneficiary. In the past, some practitioners had crafted special provisions to try to allow a Grantor to retain these types of rights, but have done so at the detriment of the aging person making the gift which later made them ineligible for Medicaid benefits.

Because the assets are held in trust by a Trustee, they can also be protected from the beneficiary's creditors, divorcing spouse, death, or bankruptcy.

Typically, we recommend there be a Trust Protector in place who is an independent third-party not related to or subordinate to the Grantor that can make limited changes to the trust if circumstances were to change in the future because the trust is irrevocable and cannot be amended by the Grantor (with limited exceptions). A Trust Protector can do things such as fill a Trustee vacancy, remove and replace a Trustee, interpret trust terms if there is a conflict or disagreement about the meaning, move the jurisdiction of the trust to another state, or grant a power of appointment to a beneficiary, for example.

The trust is structured with lifetime beneficiaries that can be anyone but just not the Grantor. It is often one or more of the Grantor's children or other family members or close friends of the family. The Trustee is appointed in the trust document by the Grantor and may be an interested Trustee who is a beneficiary of the trust or it may be an independent Trustee that is responsible for making distributions of income and principal to the lifetime beneficiaries of the trust.

How the Trust is Structured

Inside the trust, there are provisions to make the trust treated as an intentionally defective Grantor trust for tax purposes with provisions to allow a Grantor to remain living in the primary residence rent-free. The purpose of this is so that we can maintain all of the tax exemptions that go along with the primary residence for the Grantor of the trust.

An example of a tax exemption would be the federal Section 121 exclusion from capital gains on the sale of a primary residence which is a $250,000 exclusion from gain for a single person and $500,000 for a married couple (provided the Grantor resided in the residence two of the last five years prior to the sale). This can be particularly important if the primary residence needs to be sold at some point inside the irrevocable trust, but we want to get these tax benefits because the Grantor owned the property for a very long time and has a low basis in the property (which would trigger a large capital gain tax upon sale).

Since it is currently an exempt asset under California Medicaid rules, we don't have an issue with transferring the home to the trust. The Grantor can also continue to pay the property taxes and deduct them off of their tax return. However, once California enacts the proposed DRA regulations, there will be a cap on the amount of equity that is exempt for Medi-Cal qualification in the assets calculation. That amount is proposed to be somewhere between $750,000 and $828,000 for single individuals. If the home is in some of the more expensive areas of California, it could be a real problem for qualification once these new regulations go into effect. Therefore, transferring a primary residence to an irrevocable trust now would be the safest course of action.

Medicaid benefits can be applied for in California if we reserve a right to remain in the home and a right to return to the home if there is a nursing home stay.

It's very important that the Grantor never serve or have the ability to serve as a Trustee of this trust and that we have trusted family members that can be lifetime beneficiaries of the trust and can control the trust as

Trustee. We suggest that there be more than one lifetime beneficiary and that we have more than one Trustee in successive order in case anyone is unable or unwilling to serve as Trustee in the future.

During the Grantor's lifetime, the beneficiaries can withdraw money through the Trustee and those distributions can be unequal depending on how the trust as drafted. The beneficiaries can then do what they wish with those distributions but should make sure those distributions are deposited in their own personal bank accounts. If a beneficiary chooses to do so, they may use their own personal funds to help an aging parent.

After the death of the Grantor of the trust, if the personal residence is still in the trust, there will be a full step up in basis to fair market value of the home and there would be no capital gains if the property is sold shortly thereafter. That home can continue further on in trust (for added creditor protection for a beneficiary) or be distributed outright depending on the way the Grantor chooses to have the trust drafted. If the home is passed to a child beneficiary, in California, we have a parent-child exclusion which transfers the property tax basis to the child beneficiary through the County Assessor's Office.

Decanting provisions are also built in to the trust for a change in circumstances that may require a change in the structure of the trust or a change in how the trust is funded later on down the road.

Additionally, other types of assets can be funded into the trust. This may be very important for people that have other types of assets that they want to protect. However, careful planning regarding funding of the trust in this regard is required and should involve counsel from an experience Elder Law Estate Planning attorney.

The future of Medi-Cal planning for long-term care assistance is expected to change in the near future making it more difficult for an aging parent to qualify for benefits. As of the writing of this book, there have been proposed regulation changes to the qualification standards for Medi-Cal. Planning is fairly easy right now. It is strongly recommended to do planning now before the new regulations are in place as it will be more difficult to qualify at that time under the new rules. In the next chapter, we will explore the type of trust best suited for planning ahead for qualification for Medi-Cal and Veterans Aid & Attendance Pension to help in paying for the cost of long term care at home or in a skilled nursing facility when we have a veteran or a surviving spouse of a veteran.

CHAPTER NINE

What is a Veteran's Irrevocable Trust?

A Veteran's Irrevocable Trust is a type of Irrevocable Trust used in VA pension planning for long term care where we want to preserve options for both Medi-Cal and V.A. Aid & Attendance benefits. Many of the characteristics of an intentionally defective trust and a non-grantor trust have been combined into one trust under the Veterans Irrevocable Trust. Intentionally defective trusts are commonly used in high net worth planning to mitigate or eliminate estate taxes. The purpose of the trust is to protect assets from being counted for Medicaid or VA purposes and to allow lifetime beneficiaries to access trust funds as needed. Because the assets are held in trust by a Trustee, they can be protected from the beneficiary's creditors, divorcing spouse, death, or bankruptcy.

We've been able to creatively export many of the highest net worth trust planning techniques into the world of long-term care planning when we have a veteran that served during wartime to help him or his spouse to obtain benefits.

In the trust, there is no reservation of principal or income to go to the Grantor as beneficiary. In the past, some practitioners had crafted special provisions to try to allow a Grantor to retain these types of rights but have done so at the detriment of the Grantor.

Typically, we recommend there be a third-party Trust Protector in place that is not related to or subordinate to the Grantor and can make limited changes to the trust if circumstances were to change down the road. A Trust Protector can do things such as fill a Trustee vacancy, remove and replace a Trustee, interpret trust terms, move the jurisdiction of the trust to another state, or grant a power of appointment, etc.

The trust is structured with lifetime beneficiaries who can be anyone but the Grantor. It is often one or more of the Grantor's children or other family members or close friends of the family. The Trustee is appointed in the trust document by the Grantor. The Trustee maybe an interested Trustee who is the beneficiary or it may be an independent Trustee that is responsible for making distributions of income and principal to the lifetime beneficiaries of the trust.

How the trust is structured:

Inside the trust, there is a sub-trust to hold title to the primary residence and that side of the trust is treated as an intentionally defective Grantor trust. The purpose of this is so that we can maintain all of the tax exemptions that go along with the primary residence for the Grantor of the trust.

An example would be the section 121 exclusion from capital gains on the sale of a primary residence which is $250,000 for a single person and $500,000 for a married couple. This can be particularly important if the primary residence needs to be sold at some point inside the irrevocable trust but we want to get these tax benefits because the Grantor owned the property for a very long time and has a small basis in the property. If the property is sold from the Grantor's side sub-trust, the proceeds must be deposited to the Non-Grantor side sub-trust to preserve the Grantor's access to V.A. Aid & Attendance Benefits.

The Grantor side of the irrevocable trust contains provisions for allowing the Grantor to continue to live in the home rent-free until their death. Since it is currently an exempt asset under California Medicaid rules, we don't have an issue with transferring the home to the trust and it will not trigger ineligibilities. The Grantor can also continue to pay the property taxes and deduct them off of their personal income tax return.

The other side of that trust is what we call a Non-Grantor sub-trust. It has its own IRS tax identification number. If the primary residence is sold during the Grantor's lifetime, the proceeds need to be poured or funded upon sale into that Non-Grantor sub-trust.

This is a critical issue when dealing with the VA when applying for or remaining on Aid & Attendance pension. We don't want to trigger a 1099 showing the sale of the home attributed to the Grantor of the trust.

However, the purpose of having the home in the Grantor side of the trust during the Grantor's lifetime is to preserve all of the tax exemptions as well as preserve the right to remain in the home when dealing with Medicaid. Medicaid benefits can be applied for in California if we reserve a right to remain in the home and a right to return to the home if there is a nursing home stay. The home should not be rented out to third parties while it is in the Grantor trust. The reason for this is that it will trigger income to be allocated to the Grantor's tax return. The VA does check tax returns for income.

It is also very important that the Grantor never serve or have the ability to serve as a Trustee of this trust and that we have trusted family members that can be lifetime beneficiaries of the trust and can control the trust as Trustee. We suggest that there be more than one lifetime beneficiary and that we have more than one Trustee and successive order in case anyone is unable or unwilling to act in the future.

During the Grantor's lifetime, the beneficiaries can withdraw money through the Trustee and those distributions can be equal or unequal depending on how the trust as drafted. The beneficiaries can then do what they wish with those distributions but should make sure those distributions are deposited in their own personal bank accounts. If a beneficiary chooses to do so, they may use their <u>own</u> personal funds to help and aging parent with their care, comfort or medical needs not covered by Medicaid or the V.A.

After the death of the Grantor, if the personal residence is still in the Grantor side of the trust, there will be a full step-up in basis to fair market value of the home and there will be no capital gains if the property is sold shortly thereafter. That home can continue further on in trust (for added creditor protection for the beneficiary) or be distributed outright depending on the way the

Grantor chooses to have the trust drafted. If the home is passed to a child beneficiary, in California, we have a parent-child exclusion which transfers the property tax basis to the child beneficiary.

Decanting provisions are also built in to the trust for a change in circumstances that may require a change in the structure of one of the sub trusts or a change in how the sub trust is funded later on down the road.

Additionally, other non-primary residence assets can be funded into the Non-Grantor side of the V.A. trust. This may be very important for people that have other types of assets that they want to protect.

The landscape for VA pension planning for long-term care assistance is expected to change rapidly in the near future. As of the writing of this book, there have been proposed regulation changes to qualification for VA Aid & Attendance pension. It is strongly recommended to do planning now before the new regulations are in place as it will make it more difficult to qualify in the future.

CHAPTER TEN

What is a Geriatric Care Manager and Why Might One be Needed?

A Geriatric Care Manager (GCM) is a professional case manager who evaluates and assesses an elder's ability to live independently at home, helps to develop a care plan that is appropriate for them in terms of medical services and equipment and organizes their home care services as needed. They also often coordinate the aides and other medical staff that are coming in and out of the home. In addition to home care, they often manage hospitalizations and other urgent situations as well.

A professional Geriatric Care Manager is usually educated in a variety of fields, which include social work, psychology, nursing, and gerontology.

They offer support and advice for the family who is caring for their aging parent(s). The path of elder care can be a difficult and confusing one. The Geriatric Care

Manager provides expertise in many areas, helps to assess the needs of the aging parent, and provides recommendations to the family that can save time, money and many potential headaches. They can also anticipate potential issues and concerns that the family and/or the aging parent may have.

The Geriatric Care Manager can accompany the elder to doctor's appointments to assist in asking appropriate questions and treatment options and concerns. While hospitalized, the Geriatric Care Manager can keep the family informed and assist in discharge planning.

The Geriatric Care Manager's services can also be extremely helpful when the family who is caring for the elder does not live locally. They can be your eyes and ears. It provides great peace of mind to know that the Geriatric Care Manager is an advocate for your loved one. They understand the local services and are able to tap into local resources. The Geriatric Care Manager can often identify solutions to issues that may slow you down.

A relationship with a Geriatric Care Manager allows the "children to be children" while someone else manages the aging parent's care. It often helps promote a better relationship between the aging parent and their children.

ORPHAN HOLD
DO NOT SHIP

H1 – 000000000693

ISBN 9781633851207

The Smart Family's Guide to Protecting an Aging Parent fr...

CLIENT	Alternate Sourcing
STATION	TPP Receiving Station 03
HELD	2026 – 10 – 13 11:01

SHELF

If its order arrives, scan this label at a receiving station.

When you have a Geriatric Care Manager in place, it can also allow an aging parent to remain active and independent for as long as possible.

> A Geriatric Care Manager...
> ...often helps promote a better relationship between the aging parent and their children

CHAPTER ELEVEN

What do I Need to Do to Get Help?

Now that you have read this book, you have a better idea of some of the strategies and techniques to legally protect an aging parent from the ravages of a long term care financial crisis. The next thing to do is to request your meeting at our office to create a plan that best suits your situation. The aging parent should be at this meeting (if possible). It is important to make sure that they understand all the benefits and risks associated with giving away all or a portion of their assets to an irrevocable trust and the other recommended legal strategies as well. Things such as the importance of having the right type of Durable Power of Attorney for finances, an Advance Health Care Directive and a HIPAA Authorization for Release of Medical Information will be part of the discussion. You may wish to start your legal planning with a comprehensive strategy opinion letter which will give you a detailed analysis and specific recommendations for your personal situation. To schedule your appointment, please contact us at:

Geiger Law Office, P.C.
1917 Palomar Oaks Way, Suite 160
Carlsbad, CA 92008
(760) 448-2220

www.geigerlawoffice.net
info@geigerlawoffice.net

or

Law Offices of Bradley S. Erdosi
23101 Lake Center Drive, Suite 325
Lake Forest, CA 92630
(949) 261-5777

www.willsandtrustslaw.com

CHAPTER TWELVE

About the Authors

Brenda Geiger, J.D.

Managing Attorney, Geiger Law Office, P.C.

Mrs. Geiger's practice is located in Carlsbad, California. Her firm focuses on Elder Law, Estate Planning, Trust Administration, Business Planning, and Asset Protection Planning. She obtained her law degree from the University of San Diego School of Law where she served as an Editor on the board of the San Diego International Law Journal as well as published a Law Review article there.

Mrs. Geiger is involved in a variety of professional and community organizations. She serves as an editor for the North County San Diego Bar Association Magazine (The

North County Lawyer). She is also an active member of the North County Estate Planning Council and Elder Counsel, LLC. Mrs. Geiger is a frequent speaker for many national and local organizations including the North County San Diego Bar Association.

Mrs. Geiger is admitted to practice before the United States Federal Court for the Ninth District and California State Courts and is an accredited V.A. Planning Attorney. On a more personal note, she is married to Len, the CEO of a San Diego based technology company and has two children. She loves running, travel and spending time with her family.

Mrs. Geiger is also the author of several estate planning books including "Safeguarding the Nest, Third Edition", (Lulu Press, 2013) "Secrets of Great Estate Planning" (Word Association Press, 2014) and "Estate Planning Secrets of the Affluent" (Word Association Press, 2015). She has also authored the law journal article "Authorization to Kill Terrorist Leaders and Those Who Harbor Them: An International Analysis of Defensive Assassination, San Diego International Law Journal, 4

San Diego Int'l L.J. 491, Spring 2003", and several published articles on Estate Planning.

She can be reached for news interview inquires, speaking event requests and private client meetings at (760) 448-2220 or through her firm's contact page at www.geigerlawoffice.net.

Geiger Law Office, P.C.
1917 Palomar Oaks Way, Suite 160
Carlsbad, CA 92008
(760) 448-2220

www.geigerlawoffice.net
info@geigerlawoffice.net

Bradley Erdosi, J.D.

Managing Attorney, Law Offices of Bradley S. Erdosi

Bradley S. Erdosi is an attorney in Orange County, California who assists United States veterans and their surviving spouses in elder law matters, including obtaining veterans benefits and planning for long term care. The Law Offices of Bradley S. Erdosi provides comprehensive guidance and counsel in all areas of estate planning and elder law, including wills and trusts, probate, special needs and public benefits planning, community property issues, Medi-Cal planning, veterans' benefits planning and conservatorships.

Further, Mr. Erdosi is a Certified Specialist in Estate Planning, Trust and Probate Law by the State Bar of California, Board of Legal Specialization as well as an Accredited Veterans Attorney by the United States Department of Veterans Affairs. He is also a frequent lecturer on the subject of veterans' benefits, and is a regular presenter to other attorneys at continuing legal education events related to the Aid and Attendance program.

On a more personal note, Mr. Erdosi lives and works in Orange County, California and is married with two children.

For media inquiries, speaking event requests or to request a private client meeting with Mr. Erdosi, please call (949) 261-5777 or visit www.willsandtrustslaw.com.

Law Offices of Bradley S. Erdosi
23101 Lake Center Drive #325
Lake Forest, CA 92630
(949) 261-5777

www.willsandtrustslaw.com

GEIGER LAW OFFICE, P.C.
1917 Palomar Oaks Way, Suite 160
Carlsbad, CA 92008
(760) 448-2220

www.geigerlawoffice.net
info@geigerlawoffice.net

LAW OFFICES OF BRADLEY S. ERDOSI
23101 Lake Center Drive, Suite 325
Lake Forest, CA 92630
(949) 261-5777

www.willsandtrustslaw.com

WA